MW00570718

Take Your Journeys Home

Poems

Christopher Hopkins

Take Your Journeys Home $10.00
Poems by Christopher Hopkins
Clare Songbirds Publishing House Chapbook Series
ISBN 978-1-947653-12-2
Clare Songbirds Publishing House
Take Your Journeys Home © 2017 Christopher Hopkins
All Rights Reserved. Clare Songbirds Publishing House
retains right to reprint.
Permission to reprint individual poems must be obtained
from the author who owns the copyright.

Printed in the United States of America
FIRST EDITION

Clare Songbirds Publishing House Mission Statement:
Clare Songbirds Publishing House was established to
provide a print forum for the creation of limited edition,
fine art from poets and writers, both established and
emerging. We strive to reignite and continue a tradition of
quality, accessible literary arts to the national and
international community of writers, and readers. We
support our literary artists with high quality services and
on-going support. Chapbook manuscripts and art quality
poetry broadsides are carefully chosen for their ability to
propel the expansion of art and ideas in literary form. We
provide an accessible way to promote the art of words in
order to resonate with, and impact, readers not yet familiar
with the siren song of poets and writers. Clare Songbirds
Publishing House espouses a singular cultural
development where poetry creates community and
becomes commonplace in public places.

Clare Songbirds Publishing House
140 Cottage Street
Auburn, New York 13021
www.ClareSongbirdspub.com

Contents

Acknowledgements

"When the Dragon Sang and People Listened" - *The Journal* (formally the Contemporary Anglo-Scandinavian poetry), Issue #51

"Ghosts of Machinery" - *Tusk Magazine*, October 2016

"Mera Field" - *Provoke a Backlash Journal* 3, Backlash Press, September2017

"The Darkness at the Bottom of the Glass" - *Tuck Magazine*, October 2016

"Afternoon Shift Break" - *Harbingers Asylum*, Winter 2016

"Upper Mine Winter Shawl" - *Tuck Magazine*, October 2026

"Palsy Dreaming" - *VerseWright*, August 2017

"Smoke and Whiskey" - *Golden Walkman Podcast*, August 2017

"Technomediacid" - *Dissident Voice*, October 2016

"Foxes" - *Duane Poetree*, September 2016

"News Report of Trawlerman Lost" - *The Blue Nib Magazine*, September 2017

"Tuesday Night Commute" - *Rust + Moth*, Winter 2016

"Death of a Summer Flower" - *Outlaw Poetry*

"Renaming Stars" - *Blue Nib*, Issue 12, September 2017

"Take Your Journeys Home" - *Blue Nib*, Issue 12, September 2017

For Robyn Seren Hopkins

When the Dragon Sang and People Listened

You could hear the dragon sing,
when the wind blew in from the bay.

Its jewelled scales would shimmer
in the dusk and night of a summer.

Gems on the plateau,
resting before the tiger stripes of the sea.

On a magical night
its breath would catch fire,

and outshine the moon beams on the hill.
Its form stretched for miles.

They built a road alongside,
and everyone passing

always turned to the monster,
and not the purple

black and thorn
of the moon bare hills.

I knew a boy who grew up in the streets,
that were whittled out of the base rock.

Ate, slept and drank in its shadows,
under its wing,

in the timeless days
when people grew old

but the work never did.
The body itself,

was a sentinel to the town.
A forever for the faithful.

For all the hymns and quiet calling,
somehow it's breath just left,

without a mourning
or an August praise,

and grass fires are the last sparks
the hills have seen,

and funny how the ponies
are scared at night,

now there's no believing,
no ends to a tumbling loss,

and no songs sound
quite right.

Ghosts of Machinery

Ghosts of machines sit in the clouds unseen.
The giants' backs outlined,
but their shadows don't reach down
the hillside anymore.
The wildlife aren't scared off,
making homes in the ruins of toil,
while the foxes eye the street foul,
through the splinters of a bus stop at the gates.
An ex-town, a paragraph on a glossed note.
The common history,
a washed novelty
for the trickle of heritage coins.

A Sorrow on the Hill

'It's a place to go'.
Here, where nothing comes,
only the bread vans
and the 'taker.

Men drink in the lounge,
while weigh-ins for the slimmer's club go on next door.
Cigarettes left piss stains on the ceiling.
But no one's looking up.
Gaze sunk into jars upon matching
brown tables instead.

There's talk and jive,
some angered shouts.
It's a little more than drink talking
from the dark torus of the room.
Some with a rasping chest behind each line.
A crackle in the laugh,
that becomes a man's sentence.
The velvet gleam of the billiard table
is the brightest thing
in the centre of the room,
like a slice of spring in the thorn.

Money only went down the hill
in carriage,
stretched from lamp to the sea,
and it left them up there
in their houses no one wants,
longing for someone to start singing a familiar song
on a Saturday night.

Someone is to blame,
but the blame falls wrong
and nothing gets done.
All knowing that pride and lore
isn't enough,
to bay the slip of hope,
to stop the brewery locking its doors.
It was a place to go,
this place where no one comes.

Mera Field

And on the strike,
the honour bell.
That faithful ping
to sound the land,
the feel of vinyl cafe tops,
the kicks and knocks of pub door swings
and all that lines the blunt peach stones.

A war dead thanks chimes in the air,
above the pound shop till ring din.
For those boys,
once lambs,
the farness gone,
like the fading leaf of wrought iron curve,
under years of lick of council paint,
on the resting place of the brass band's song.

Trace your fingers across the names.
Their gilded edge from the seasons touch,
against the black brass plaques to the fallen man.
Names still called in classroom shouts,
and amongst the team sheet nods.

While dark the soul of this country's heart,
how would the ghosts now see this land?
As the reason they endured hell,
or as black
as the murder grounds on which they fell.
Such surrender in this no man's land,
this losing war on blunt peach stones.
Hope and strength,
now unthinkable loads.

Gone the youth,
once blind on destiny,
now the young
blinded with allegories,
of food bank opportunities.
The poor callow fools of self.

And the old like unwanted books,
bent double from the wounds unseen,
tight lipped and cold,
and hearts, not lungs, silted up like coal.

Life is death
and death holds all.
All in this hideous familiar.

The pointed bell shrills,
with such savage discipline,
the simple peal as a devils gun,
sounding out the roundabouts
and flag poles bare,
the café tops and hairdressers chairs,
the white goods
and red faces,
the betting shops
and the charity whores,
who stand behind their glass counters.
And the graveyards worn thin,
tended by natures hand,
and council strimmers hymn.

Then the last strike of the hammered chime,
sounds the shot that killed the poet dead,
and it brings the air
to a shattered peace,
a senselessness,
like a covering pall,
on the lace doilie houses
to the rotting town hall.

There will be no prayers,
no torch held high,
no chimes or bells for these quiet lives.
None shall be remembered,
in this town pronounced dead.
For the best
it is said.

The Darkness at the Bottom of the Glass

Don't think it switches on,
with another Friday night drink.
The animals sinking jars to stop the rising disaffection.
Then the countdown of the walk home.

The urgency in horror.

Don't think it's something
which controls him.
Makes him walk the line
then drags the brood ragged.

It's always there.

Sometimes it wears a tie
and buys the milk.
Picks up the kids on time,
and loves in his own way.

It's always there.

Those crocodile eyes at the waters edge.
Snap, snap, snap.

You know that relief,
when the wildebeest gets away?
Yet you know the leathered jaws
will still kill to feast.

Those behind the silent doors,
canned lipped and curtains closed,
tonight brings a pitiful anticipation.

Don't think it's the darkness from the drink,
that drives this animal to lunge.
Don't dare feel anything for him.

A Lamb Walks Under Parking Signs
on the Main Street After Dark

She lives on an island where the asphalt meets
the Atlantic.
With the mountains behind her,
and the street light switch,
hums lullabies every night.
Her thoughts came out of her head like tree roots,
when she wasn't trying
to fold them away,
and her spit,
it tasted of that sea.
Tiny hickeys of threaded stigmata
on the white of her arms,
spelling out her Gemini's.
Trace lines and star signs,
and the occasional thick lip goodbye.

She is a portrait of the night.
It holds her hand
as much as the glimmer-time holds her up right.
Contours of her hips, like arrows to the limelight.
She becomes the desire line.
The apple
but turning on the orchard floor.
She walks the forgiving line.
Weighed down on back seats of chance,
bruised lines of finger grips, her Sergeant stripes,
with bad luck on her shoulder, whispering oks,
like a pimp of promise which never comes.
A lamb walks under parking signs,
on the main street after dark.
Sits under war paint in the bathroom light.
Jesus hangs on a silver link,
shivers in the passing beams.

The Snake Pit of Factory Lights on the Black Canal

The kids eat.
Father works
and mother works harder,
counting coppers.
Pride is not a sin.
Pride means worth.
Worth means love and a future.
No resignation from duty,
from the Monday mornings
of responsibilities.
All this, is for love.

Afternoon Shift Break

Neck bucked.
Face raised
up to the apricot touch.
The afternoon falling
between metal stairwell steps
as if your lover
tracing fingers
warm across the brow and cheek
in a docile moment between the sheets.
Back rests against the hook brick wall.
Knees wombed and arms willowed over.
The monochrome tip of a cigarette
rustle lava glow on the intake at the lips.
Fresh air and tobacco
all as one.

Upper Mine Winter Shawl

Days as different,
as different as the colours of bone and mud.
A weathered carcass of hill pony,
solid in its misadventure,
rests amongst the waves of a sweeping mallow tide.
Here, at the vale's black watermark,
fortunes fleet with the ebb away of the Mother's breath.
Even on September eves,
of Venus and the moon,
there waits a whispered chill,
and soon, the Norther points to a deeper cold.
Then the turning comes
and the land is put to death.
And on the rough tides,
of the ploughed mountain side,
the scarring of beauty never sleeps,
as the compass bars of draglines swing,
to the brim heart toil at the black tar pit.
Fuel oil bangs ring out,
like a drumming of it's fractured beat.
And at the town's border scree,
smoke ambles to the pale slung heavens,
up from the sheltering lines of stone cots below,
spanning like the finger bones of a dirt creased hand,
with that palm of work at its ridge.
And in those doilie houses made of stone,
where the meals are taken
and washing lines banners that buck in the wind,
the loving brood wait out the hours,
'til all come down from the hill,
safe to the native hearths.
And as the fracture lines are worked by hand,
cracks appear in the season's run.
And slow, the Mother's breath does come,
and life, life unlocks itself
in the turning back to living waters.
Then under late moon smile,
as a mallow tides cover the short thorn hills,
the pieced land still bleeds black,
from a scar that just won't be healed,

until the word comes and the ledges are closed,
quicker than a seasons close.
Those stone homes,
become as hollow as the weathered bone,
as a winter shawl falls for good.

Palsy Dreaming

Your invented life,
never came back home.
The front door still open,
to your little refugees.
The hall is now black
as the wet slate roof,
and your chapel's stone grows colder.
Dust foams on
the floorboard's worn form,
from the sermons shuffling feet
of standing room only.

The walk to the school
was only up the hill.
Learnt the poetry of pierced sides,
heart and blood
hung on rhythm and rhyme.
All of the majesty,
held up by voce and blue stencilled columns.
All that truth would be shaken to life
by the grey pin stripped master himself.
Even the town drunk tipped their ears,
bathed and baptised by spit.

When the new college came
it took the best,
and with it a town's anaemic breath.
Bramble grew thick and fast,
while decisions hang like washing lines.
A way of living and a way of death,
with it's finger nails in the skins of yesterday's,
and streets that grow quiet with age.
They'll never come back.
They have their own lives now,
away from the palsy dreaming.

Still Born of the Reincarnated

The earth is still black,
in this place of your birth,
only now the council does the digging.

No hammering loads,
on the stepped hill.
Only the cemetery rock needs heaving.

Swept it all under the carpet,
under the new contours of the vale.
They put the top back on,

called back the birds,
put flowers amongst the thorny grasses,
all, on that green bandaged hill.

And when Merak's point of blackened share,
tries to part the land in our dreaming,
down from the haul road the footsteps come,

the new life to the stoic comes.
The noise of the nightly bin men,
crying calls to their beauties from the lanes,

brings us all to our windows twitching.
See, they comes to lick the old life still,
and we see more kick in the fox's tail

than in any of our morning ways,
and all the quiet dreaming that lives in prays,
like our stories, now play dead.

And of the dawn we hear the bird song calling,
not the ring of a shift change hymn.
And tear comes, and I don't know why.

I cry just the same.
Lay the flowers on the grave,
of blooms picked from upon the hills.

Land of Loss and Dreaming

Continents of patterned colour,
mapped to apples in the fruit bowl.

The kitchen is tidy for once.
While maggots,

turn to flies in the neighbours bins.
Front room view

of a laundry horse
and TV catch up habits.

Our four walled romancing.
Happy are us few,

to understand our meaning,
in this land of loss and dreaming.

Winter Moths

The shadows of the street lights swing with the commute.
Flared sienna yellow,

between the watercolours pooling black.
Us winter moths of January,

move off the frantic ways.
Over stopping lines,

feel the ode to joy of a parking space,
the lucent light of chiller aisles,

to our private lives behind closed doors.
And all the while the wolf moon waits,

above our forest walls,
where desire lines are turning black,

upon the tip jar covering,
and up the 'skelters of ivy sheen,

to the electric black of the oak trees bare,
the starving eyes stare the twilight dying,

the hunter's teeth tears in
moon beam smiles.

Diesel trains muscle into sunken towns.
Us, all tinned meat unloading,

with a hurried pace for such grazing stock,
along the flagstone's numbered stops.

Stepping light, onto our forest tracks,
with a thug embrace of gale force warnings

to blow us home,
what ever the shape our sails may be,

to our cathedrals of living.
The closed rooms where our freedoms be,

away from storms they give names to.
Our flicker of life in the light of the moon.

Smoke and Whiskey

A warm rasp
of bullet tipped fingers on violin,
of a nylon six string hum,
and the brushing of a side drum.

Honeycomb light,
nursing the mood
    and tempo between the walls.
We drink from short glasses.
Eyes of black in the electric glow.

Time capsuled,
until the closing bell calls for taxis,
and out with the current of the crowd we go.
Our watchfires of certainty,
flicking out their tongues
to taste the night.

Us smiling,
with secrets of the womb we made there.
Secrets we'll take home,
place on the shelf like pine cones,
and look to,
    when the weather 'comes too much.

Technomediacid

the electric fog
keeps me from sleep

my head
amongst the clouds

holding hands
with the zeros and ones

staring down
the electron gun

Foxes

And the foxes know more about me than
google.

Every night their black socks
and moustaches in the trash.

The oxide wash
under the satellite slipway,
sailing the darkness,
between the scaffolding streetlight beams.

They cluck and bark as they talk about me.
Sharing gossip on the breeze with their watcher grace.

Pizza twice in a week,
nosing the folds of boxes.
The overdraft bigger than last month,
and the price of gas up again,
chewed over crumpled logos.

'He's always pulled from the shores
by the drowning moon',
they tattle the modern turn of heartache and heart attack.
'There is no architecture
 to his silent living'.
They shake their heads,

They look towards my door,
a look
only a mother could give,
a fox bite from love's fanged lip,
that promise
of the gentle perfection of worry.

My heart mulls it over,
remembering the living.
They would miss me dearly.

Office Collection for a Colleague's Passing

The snows came down
on the eastern tail.
River veins in the white by dawn.

Rise,
the tracing paper sun.
Above the rush,

above the done.
The bloodless bow,
on the black bed muds,

untroubled.
The folded crease in manila brown,
as the tidal brim to the river's crown.

Coins fall and chime.
Sympathy and coffee,
and a patent leather shine.

The Last Time the Ground Will Give

The daylight has aged.

Time has been called by the nature of things.

The sky did build its temper,
and howled in breaking.

Then the earths firm to clays
idle under sun and nail.
All the vigour of the term
soaked up in the flesh and grain.

Skins on the lip of bleaching,
wait for the tiger charred crates
to be stacked by the heavy limbs.
Silk heads of wheat have been taken in.
The stubbled crowns wait to be turned.
But I hear no share will break the ground this year.
No dragging boards,
no folds to air,
no crows to pick the worms.

There's silver bones of starveling volts,
stilted and hammock strung,
now loom over wasp tanned diggers,
where blue diesel genies run,
and the crows,
and the crows,
who don't care where the worms come from.
Tank hard and shovelled hands,
turning up the down to the blue paper plans.
An authentic view to tempt desire,
along the cul-de-sac brass letter boxes
and furniture overtures to come.
The blossom scents from washing lines,
and greenhouse fruits that rot on the vine.

News Report of Trawlerman Lost

It is a welcome sight,
only known to them,
hooker and line.
The lights of the pub
and the quay side chapel
shine out to the dark,
where the salt grey reaches.

Horizon sat stars,
guiding the hearts back home,
to the hillside fortresses of family arms.
Today, that home-come relief
is cold at the sight of these pricks of light.

The kindred gather at the shoreline breaking,
as a silence drowns the pitching surf,
they look to the offing like driftwood rooted,
waiting for the answer to the harrowed asking,
whose prayers have been forsaken?

And the answer comes on a cert of bobs,
on the steamily slow course bow.
The engine sounds clack out loud,
like the hooves of a pale horse messenger.

'Come quickly home, come safely so',
 were the singing graces for the leaving crew.
Now whispering pleas in grasped amens,
'Lord, don't leave my love forsaken'.
Then the halt of beat upon the mark,
brunt knuckle white around the heart,
as the name is said, so softly so.
Sorrow for the loss and a good man too.

And waves roll down on that hollowed soul.
The wash of grief through the cockle shell floor.
The spindrift tears touch the lips,
and the taste is of a man's last breath.

Through the calling hours of curtains closed,
wake beers bought in lieu of flowers,
their prayer hands still clasped together,
as they're told, with hands on heart,
'The voice of the Lord is upon the waters'.
Guilt in relief,
the end for others.

30th March at the Sea

We move forwards. Backwards.
Guided by chewing gum constellations, .
to the happy marriage in feathered grey;
the sky
and the sea.

Jaundiced sands and kite wire winds,
cross cutting the salt debris,
the itch of identity, rooted in the span,
this coffin by the sea.

The only potential,
is in the olive swell,
or a threat of a change of wind
to an unreal smile,
in this place of come and go,
of the gentle work of gravity.

The tides, come and go,
like the room spaces
in the old peoples home,
stinking of death,
of what the ebb leaves behind.
That stickiness of unclean.

And in the sheltering arcades,
to the sounds of tin and pennies,
yesterday's headlines are soaked in vinegar and glee,
forgetting that they called the rock salmon a dog fish,
while Jesus is dismissed by the Pharisees.

Now, the turn over of cooling fans,
above the bingo call voters,
in their fading cinema hall glam,
hums,
like the conch shell tinnitus
of a deafness proud,
over these, the new boarders,
of this doleful pleasure land.

Tuesday Night Commute

That cataract haze,
just past sundown.

March is shaking Winter's hand
goodbye.

Only a cuff of moon above,
gloriously perfect.

The switch of street lights,
a sodium pink,

now the day has truly gone.
Rushes of brick fronts

and the guard dog teeth of rose bushes
dout the work day's wick.

Porch light phare,
teases with promise,

of the bless'ed comfort waiting.
     The loving.

Familiar veins on the concrete path,
my map to guide me home.

Night Rover

The fish hook lights,
ex'd in their standing
burning yellow bait.

Staggered in the course,
like picked ribs stood
on a wet flensing stage.

The emptiness burning softly,
above the rushes
of the marrow and the blood,

the to and fro,
along the silver spine,
the monster's innards hollowed out.

My onward moves
in straight lines,
with the back end canvas

of a white van in front.
Framed to one side,
the glare of the white marrow rush,

to the other,
                the dark bracken,
where the wild dogs wait.

Daydreaming in Sleep

Coal dust settles on the evening.
On the little town,
and its joins between others.
The back roads and backyards quieten,
less the calling for a dog
that never comes.

The night grows with the night sounds.
The tyre drum on sandpaper streets.
The hum of a white moth's drive
under scaffolding lights.
The volume of a moment,
filling the space in its passing.
Then the quietness of nothings.

There's a stubbornness of sunlight in the stars.
Running a million miles,
leaving so many years ago,
to be here, witnessing tonight,
as moons start flaming in window frames,
the blue tint on concrete paths.
We think nothing of it,
their journeys burning
like a million TV boxes bright.
Picture tuned.
Too small to see.

And the night grows from exterior in.
The tides of street lights and roof line blue,
are as the darkness under a breaking wave,
to the moonlit top of the cresting fall.
Then the night swallows this town whole.
This little town dark.
Sleeping in the shadows of chandeliers.
In the ozone perfume of sprinklers,
after the crack and shudder.
Residents disappear
into slumber after prayers,
of asking well of the dead.

Blood Orange Cry

It's not until September,
you notice the salmon lanterns
in the twilight.

The darkest green in profile trees,
and stout lines
of roof tops in the west.

The sun-fall breaks your heart.
It's bruising line
from the fire

folding under its own weight.
The blood orange cry,
to the youngling blue.

As the warmth leaves
the bodies and the earth,
you'll find the leaves will yield by dawn.

Death of a Summer Flower

Honeysuckle trash
across the lawn,
as how the handfast blossom
shivers
from lichgate to porch.

Gone the wild night,
between the thick of summer,
and this sober morn.

The songbird and her bough,
still dazed
from elbow and fist,
of untimely skies,
from the rough grey hands of God.

Renaming stars

A sea of ancient deity.
The forever evolving things.
Our sky of burning dust.

We named them as gods
and from their place we found our way,

while the whitening eye of a moon
touches its numb light on all the living,

and how some buds flower by the moon,
while the others wait for the wash of morn
to let their colours come.
How Nyx has been forgotten,
and the stars are renamed as other things.
The forever evolving things.

Our flash of life,
this very moment,
hurtled into space at speed,
and light years away.

One day,
maybe we will catch them up.
Running faster than light can take,
and walk amongst our days again.
To look upon ourselves,
by the light of stars and moon.
Wonder how we found our way.
How we didn't even know their names.

Take Your Journeys Home

No words to spark the lightning.
Bolt fire skies
at shutter speed.

The thunder crack roll away,
away,

    and I can't tell,
      if the tumbling blare is heaven,

or the infrasound of the jewel line,
dual bound.

A slowing S.O.S.
of rain from the gutter spill,
as the storm takes its journey home.

        Away, away.

The Old Know and the Young Suspect

The wind changed and
blunted the song
with its sally and rush.
We see the faces left,
mouthing nothings.

The tune fades in for a beat
behind a lull in the wind,
but the passage can't be placed
to words we know.
Gone is the word of promise.

Certainties

The linen was hung out grey.
Folding over itself on the wind.
Our roof sky, our land,
the colour as the rocks that made the stone
of that sharp cheerless face of the chapel.
A million years of history pushed death and time as hard
as the spike that split it from the earth.
Gods creatures, Triassic non-believers, seeded in the stone.

Standing tall in the soot green,
though it's language was no chameleon of the town.
The windows panes, a river bed dull.
Only in prayer
did the revere of a scenes come true.
Only in the candlelight room did we see the Boy glow.
Us, cut off from the outside,
stories lit from behind by the world you couldn't see.
Which ever side of the walls you stood,
never did the other show.
Strange how they kept their beauty for their own.

You only ever saw one side of the august preacher.
He knew the need for an outpouring of sorts.
The way he spoke made ladders into the Book.
Us all listening with acute dog ears,
and we saw the sacrifice
in every fence and telephone pole, going home.
In the drinking rooms there's talk of dubiety
with crossed fingers stuffed into pockets,
thinking it was the Lord's breath on the wind,
the Ghost's breath on your neck.
Our hearts had gone to the head
and cut off the thinking.

Looking into the Shadows on Llewellyn Street

Climbing the hills
leaves a breathlessness in chest.
Reaching the high of heaven's first step.
The whitebait coloured streets,
a wishing uncommonness in the doilied
rows in our glare of noon.

In lilac and rust, the land,
matching the width of sea.
Eye, caught the line of the carriageway
from east and west,
to the whirl-pooling slip roads,
screwed down into the belly of town.

All set in light and dark,
all divided in the silver,
with the shimmer crown
against the brine tide breaking,
and a sky's beaked egg shell blue.

Lift up the shadows on Llewellyn Street.
Peal back the liquorice stencil map
and use the flooding light to look
into the blood of our own love,
wrapped in brick, prayer and paper.

In the white sun,
see the burden of the shadow men,
pooling in rooms of drink and doubt,
where the future only goes as far
as the Christmas coming.

The blood turning fat in chest and arms,
like a sea reclaiming it's land.
On their crutches in mind, until all they taste is the brine
in a dreaming embrace of the purging flood,
thickened with our sinners
panting bitter luck.

The longing for purpose,
like the want of plastic bags that ride the oceans dreaming,
ghosts of use, ghosts of men.
Spirts downed and drowned for good,
set under lilac hills,
and the rust from salt burning.

Christopher Hopkins grew up on a council estate in Neath, South Wales during the1970's. This fractured landscape of machines and mountains and the underlying 'Hiraeth' in Welsh life has developed into a distinctive voice and soul in his poetry. He currently resides in Canterbury and works for NHS cancer services.

Christopher has had poems published in *Backlash Press*, *The Journal* (formally the Contemporary Anglo – Scandinavian poetry), *Rust & Moth*, *Harbinger Asylum*, *Scarlet Leaf Review*, *Anti-Heroin Chic*, VerseWrights, Tuck Magazine, Dissident Voice magazine, Poetry Superhighway, Duane's PoeTree, Outlaw Poetry. Christopher's spoken word poetry has also featured in a podcast of Golden Walkmen Magazine. Two of his early e-book pamphlets "Imagination Is My Gun" and "Exit From A Moving Car" are available on Amazon.